Journals for Everyone

Journals For Everyone
ISBN-13: 978-1986963312
ISBN-10: 1986963314

Made in the USA
Monee, IL
24 July 2020

36941555R00056